# Lines

TAHIR HUSSAIN

Dedicated to my Dad

I miss you beyond what words can say.

Until we reunite in light.

A blank page is a doorway to infinite possibilities.

Deep down every poet is leaving behind a trail to his or her soul.

I've learnt the secret of writing beautifully

Is thinking beautifully.

If the whole world was plagued with blindness

We'd have nothing to fall in love with

*Except kindness.*

Feelings are temporary,

But how you made someone else feel—

Now, that's permanent.

Love is keeping the bird cage open.

Loving you was like watering a wildflower.

Loving you was dousing myself in gasoline

*But incinerating from within.*

I guess I'm a good poet because I feel too much, too
intensely, and all too soon.

People
Like waves
Come and go


And just like the waves
You only remember the ones that had the biggest impact

Loving an artist

Is

Loving madness

Memories and experiences

Were the currencies of the soul

*And I wanted to die wealthy.*

Be the rare creature

That drinks all the poison

*But still spills honey.*

You might spend an eternity not knowing love is the biggest fear you must conquer.

Choose the love that leaves you lighter
Less like someone else and more like you

Her beauty was not a look, it was a feeling.

Most writers

Use complicated words for simple meanings

I use simple words to describe complicated feelings

*That's the difference.*

5 days Craving, 2 days bingeing—

*You*

Kisses like sugar, Christmas without snow

Passionate hearts, drunk in love

Know no sorrow.

Underneath our art

We were just children
In love with love
With colors and with words.

Magic with you,

Madness without.

Nothing like hot chai on a rainy day,

Thinking of a lost love
To really get the words out.

Last night's shirt on her chest
Hair ruffled up; she was moving on my lap.
Rays on her skin, eyes on each other

*Lips closing in on the gap*

Men must have a bad boy's mind and a good boy's heart

With a tongue that's somewhere in between.

Kiss her where her jaw meets her neck
Bite her where her arm meets her breast

*"No way," I* told her

I'd let her stay dressed.

Like insects we scurried into our concrete hives and
stayed there
Unable to face a micro threat

Nature gently reminding us our debt

*On Covid*

Don't validate her feelings as right or wrong,

Feelings are truth in the moment.

It was not that she was not sensual,

She just knew how to hide it well.

In messy bedrooms with messy hearts
Let's make love so perfect

My heart is aroused at
The road less travelled
At the thoughts of unknown lands
Watching sunsets only a handful have witnessed
With a hand holding my hand

Listen to my heart and find my voice
Let's love so bright
Like we have no choice

A diamond deserves another, so shine like one.

A perfect symphony of the universe you are

The most perfectly aligned set of atoms.

A soul burning with passion,

*Heals any broken heart*

And the strongest of winds can move the
widest of clouds,
And the smallest of rains can quench the
driest of deserts.

What's a broken heart that some self-love
can't fix?

Empty bottle, empty hearts,

Souls full of memories.

And she conveyed
More with a peck on his cheek
In front of her home
Than he could ever interpret
From a sneaky make-out in a shady lane.

Anjuna to Ashvem
On a motorcycle on a whim
Beer and laughter
Till the sun goes dim.

Aren't our souls made of fire?

Because sparks fly every time our eyes collide.

Attraction could be with anything

But seduction is always with the eyes.

Flower behind her ear
Flower on her fingers
Miles away
Yet her thought lingers

A thousand kisses
In a few hours
You so close
And the world so far

After many seasons
After many moons
Her notification

Still I swoon.

And all I have are dreams and words

*She sets both ablaze.*

And with only a few moments,
She made him fly.
She made him feel,

So much so that he could write a book.

*Only if she turned to look.*

He could see her to her depths.

What walls?
What layers?
What puzzle?

Why does sinning feel so poetic?

I felt it in the sunset,
I felt it in the sunrise
I'm now living on hopes,

For a love that has no demise.

I look at you

Like how a Man is supposed to *look* at his Woman.

Our safe word was a look.

One glance,
One touch,
One whisper,
One kiss,

And in those moments, they became one.

Reaching out and kissing her

Felt like reaching out and kissing the moon.

Red marked souvenirs on the skin.

Cold weather, 100 feet road, hugs,
I kissed the lips of you
Whiskey, brandy, beer jugs,

Now I'm home,
Left with the taste of you

She was a rose, with petals like infinite layers.

You couldn't tell where one started and where one ended.

Fragile.

She was a feeling to be felt.

If I could play my life back like a movie tape,

I wish every frame has you in it.

Out at a bar and I saw you

Hair flip

Well-proportioned miracle

20% unattainable,

80% irresistible.

I'd break a thousand cages, just to see you fly once.

I still feel your lashes on my lips,

And your fingertips on my soul,

Your tight grip as you shuddered


When we became whole.

I spent my 20s making memories, the 80-year-old me will smile about.

I love like my poems—small, intense doses, sandwiched between nothingness.

I guess the end game is to love yourself so hard, that no one else could possibly compete.

I fail to believe that when we kiss for the first time, we don't just leave scents over each other but also a fraction of our soul.

Hugs and kisses were her water and sunlight to her bloom.

How others treat you is how you treat them.
How others treat you is a sum of their insecurities,
traumas, fears, morals, values *and* how you treat them.

How do you know the difference if she's doing it for you or if she's doing it because she can't help herself?

*The music from her lips.*

His heart and feet roamed like the world belonged to him.

Her lips tasted of cigarettes, alcohol, and adventure.
My lips—sober, pink, and cautious.

*The roles were definitely reversed.*

He wrote a thousand words, but she always read between the lines.

He moved with time itself.
Fire in his eyes,
Ache in his heart.

He found comfort in her, no home could provide.

Give me a forever lover, and I will forever write.
During chilly nights,
During crazy fights,
During our travels,
While our clothes unravel,
After our drunken adventures,
When one of us is sick and the other is tender,
I promise you'll be my centre.
Give me a forever lover.

Girl,
If you can't find reasons beyond his looks, status, and
bedroom skills to love him, *don't.*
That's not love, and that boy deserves so much more.

Flooded sheets,
Flushed cheeks,

*Midnight snacks.*

Easy to fall in love with.
Hard to love.

Don't dim your light because others are too used to darkness, and you're blinding them.

Choose wisely who you share your soul with,
Because once you do, it's gone for good, and that takes its
own toll too.

There's nothing purer than the dreams of a girl madly in love.

The cruellest thing I wouldn't do is to know a girl who is
hurt
And hurt her even more.

You wanted me with haste,
Kisses sweet but soul black,

Leaving nothing but an aftertaste.

Kissed a lot of princesses that turned out to be frogs.

Traffic is the cost of good friendships in Bangalore & Mumbai.

She said she wanted to explore everything
Experience everything
I wish someone told her


I am a human being.

*Not an experience.*

Telling her she's Beautiful,

And making her *feel* Beautiful,

Are two very different things.

She spoke non-stop for 20 minutes

And all I heard was
4 laughs
3 eye rolls
3 hair flips

And the constant smile on her lips

The gut knows whose views are love and admiration and whose views are just Nazar.

Soft souls,

Need space to bloom.

Riding an Enfield in Goa is poetry in and of itself.

My moon is too bright for your night

My sun too large for your darkness

If you offer bandages for a wound that is within

I will never ask you for bandages again.

I will quickly discount you

If you tell me your Kindness has a price

So you can sell yourself your own delusions

And buy for yourself your own sweet lies.

For the blind— clinging on to passing rays, makes sense.

What's love,

But bridges between souls?

The sun is surrounded in darkness

But does the darkness ever envelop the sun?

You count the distance travelled by the body in miles

You count the distance travelled by the soul in years.

Some people bend reality itself with the force of their will.

Every man has both a God and a Beast inside him,

Most women push him towards only one over the other

Only few inspire both out of him.

If words didn't sway women,

Smut and Romance novels would be out of business.

My soul is a thirst trap.

I belonged to the divine feminine

And she was everyone,

*And no one at the same time.*

I look to impress only two people in my life


The little boy, decades behind me

The wise old man, decades ahead of me.

Don't expect to grow a garden on barren ruins.

We bartered our sleep
For dreams
That we witnessed
With our eyes wide open.

Teach me your native tongue

I want you to feel like you are *home* when you talk to me.

Sometimes all you need is warm hugs and sweet words

Like kheer for the soul.

Show me an inch of your skin that I haven't kissed

Show me an inch of your soul that I haven't loved.

Pink sunsets
Purple skies
Green lands
Black hearts—

*Attempting white love.*

Let my words be as soft as a butterfly's flap

Even in the face of a thousand tornadoes

*They still matter.*

Real love is kindness set on fire.

The broken heart is twice shy
Its walls thrice high

She was art none of my words could describe
I was her muse none of her colours could capture

So we came closer

To leave behind the smell of her acrylics on my skin
While I leave behind my poems and sonnets on your soul


*On artists in love*

Who are poets?

But minds, voices and words distilled in a soul

That sets a generation on fire.

When you're done building your kingdom, you'll know the difference between pretty damsels that need chasing and queens who will stay behind and protect it.

Never underestimate the power of words

It was the words "I have a dream" that set a race free

It was the words "An eye for an eye" that brought our colonial predators to heel.

And when you compare the pen with a sword

You'll know that one can only vanquish

The other is

*Immortal*

Your soul

Is light
Burn it so bright, that it fuses.

Your soul

Is Sound
Screech it at its highest frequency – Deafening and
consistent.

Your soul

Is an Engine—
Red line it.

I crave you like the river craves the sea
Travelling mountains and conquering valleys
To meet you with a gush

*Unable to escape the rush.*

When you see a good deed done
Why do you hold back your kind words and show
indifference instead?

And then ask if your kind words are something that really
matters,
If it is something that I should chase or if I am seeking
your validation?

No.

I wasn't seeking your validation
I was seeking your kindness

And in this process of your indifference
*You have lost mine*

That was the way of passion

Feelings first

Questions later.

If my light ever seemingly flickers

I will watch you intensely on what you do next

Scramble to hold the wires together

Or leave them vexed.

I am the voice of the unheard

Of the mute
Of the underdog
Of the forgotten

I am the voice
For the cogs of your wheel
The thorn on your heel

I am light, refracting. Compounding.

What most people don't get is

78 kgs of brawn, brains and bravado

Is still protecting the soul of a 10-year-old boy

And it will always remain so.

Music and art are the result of talented hands

Theatre is the result of a talented face

Science is the result of a talented mind

Poetry is the result of a talented soul.

The Divine masculine and the Divine feminine

Are nothing but masks of our ideals, opposite to our own
sex.

Don't go put these immortal holy masks on mortal human
demons.

The best way to befriend a dog is to throw it a bone

The best way to befriend a lion—is to share the kill.

Our kids see

More beautiful faces in a day
Than the kings did a mere 200 years ago

And that we're living today in Heaven

Or hell.

Depends on who you ask.

Some of you could compete with an infant for your need
for attention.

If you want to live in a fortress, start building strong walls.

I wish I had many sisters

Because passionate love is
Always a war with the other

But women go to wars,
If it comes to their brothers.

Beauty and Success are the polarity that spins modern civilisation.

Beauty wants Success
And Success wants Beauty.

One doesn't feed validated enough, without the other.

A simple mating strategy that birthed competition and capitalism.

Solitude is to poets
What coal is to fire

My poetry blurred into my prayers
My prayers blurred into my poetry.

If you ever saw the Divine in me,

Know – that it is the Divine in you,

Reflecting back.

*I just cleaned the mirror.*

Tahir Hussain (born 23 November 1992, Bangalore, India) is a celebrated Indian poet known for his evocative and concise style of writing. His poetry, which gained widespread recognition on Instagram, delves into themes of passionate love, the dualities of life, and the rapidly shifting ideologies of India's digital "swipe" generation.

Blending heartfelt observations with a modern perspective, Tahir's work resonates deeply with readers navigating the evolving intersections of technology, relationships, and identity in contemporary India.